CODEPENDENCY

Balancing an Unbalanced Relationship

JUNE HUNT

AspirePress

Torrance, California

Codependency: Balancing and Unbalanced Relationship
Copyright © 2013 Hope For The Heart
All rights reserved.
Aspire Press, a division of Rose Publishing, Inc.
4733 Torrance Blvd., #259
Torrance, California 90503 USA
www.aspirepress.com

Register your book at www.aspirepress.com/register
Get inspiration via email, sign up at www.aspirepress.com

Printed in the United States of America
011212DP

CONTENTS

ear friend,

I hate to admit it. I wish it weren't true. But I know what it's like to have been a "closet codependent." (Actually, those closest to me knew it, even if they didn't know the word *codependent*.)

In my heart of hearts, I know what it's like to compromise my conscience in order *to comply*, to be a "peace-at-any-price" person in order *to appease*, to put up with chaos in order *to avoid conflict*. Although I myself had not heard of "codependency," I found myself in an exhilarating, yet fearful relationship, full of highs and lows—in a roller-coaster relationship with continual ups and downs, but I did not know how to get off the ride!

In truth, even though I knew *something* in the relationship was wrong and *something* needed to change, I was desperately "needy" of connection and deathly fearful of rejection. When my "friend" would threaten to leave, I would beg, plead, and promise *whatever was necessary* in a desperate attempt to stay connected. My immense fear of being abandoned led me into a long season of insecurity. At that time, I viewed my loyalty as noble. Today, I see my loyalty as excessive.

By prioritizing exclusive loyalty to a person, I relinquished my highest loyalty to the Lord.

Sadly, I didn't know that these high/low swings were not "normal." After all, that destructive dynamic was part of *my normal*—the normal, volatile relationship I witnessed between my parents. Because Dad had threatened to put Mother in a mental institution, each day when I came home from school, I never knew whether she would be at home or sent away. Dad would often say to me, "*Your mother is mentally ill today.*" Every time he said those words *my blood would boil*. The problem was this: I knew he had the money and the power *to pay off a psychiatrist*! Fortunately, every psychiatrist who evaluated Mother told him that she was not mentally ill. But his continued efforts petrified both Mother and me and left both of us terribly insecure. Such is the breeding ground for codependency.

Loyalty to my mother became the highest priority in my life. Even if it meant lying, I had to protect her. I had a never-spoken commitment: "If we are both thrown out of the house, I will 'sweep streets' (literally) to pay for a little apartment and buy enough food to keep us alive." Somehow, I would take care of Mother. Ultimately, I felt responsible for her welfare, and it was "do or die." (I would do it or die.) In truth, we had a role reversal.

Later, when I became an adult, I found myself having *excessive loyalty*—"excessive" because my highest loyalty was to a person, not to the Lord. I was controlled more by my fear in a friendship than by my faith in Christ. Without even knowing it, I had let a person take the place that the Lord alone should have had.

To move away from that codependent dynamic was more difficult than I ever imagined, and it took longer than I ever dreamed, but oh, was it worth the effort—and the pain.

What indescribable peace when we learn that our security is in the Lord and when our own relationships are right in God's sight! I know, because today I am truly free.

If you've ever struggled with loving a person more than God, this book is for you. Through its pages, you'll discover how to get out from underneath the "trapped" feeling that has plagued you for so long. You'll learn never to settle for what *looks* good, but always to choose what *is* best. And as you go, you will have my sincere prayer that the Lord will create in you an undivided heart with complete dependence on Him—a new heart to set you free to live without fear—a pure heart for you to become the person He created you to be.

Yours in the Lord's hope,

June
June Hunt

*"Create in me a pure heart, O God,
and renew a steadfast spirit within me."*
(Psalm 51:10)

CODEPENDENCY
Balancing an Unbalanced Relationship

When God gave us His Ten Commandments, He began with these words, *"You shall have no other gods before me"* (Exodus 20:3). He knew that if we would make our relationship with Him our top priority, He would bless our lives, and, through our other relationships, we would be a blessing to others.

The primary problem with codependency is that it violates the heart of God's first commandment. In a codependent relationship, you allow someone else to take the place that God alone should have in your heart. You allow another person to be your "god." If you have a *misplaced dependency*, you will have neither *peace with God* nor the *peace of God*. But if you put the Lord first, living each day *dependent on Him*, you will have God's peace, even when others are not peaceful toward you. This is one reason God says to us...

> "You shall have
> no other gods before me."
> (Exodus 20:3)

9

DEFINITIONS

Imagine that you have been handpicked by God to impact all the people around you. You have been *chosen* to be the liberator throughout the land, *chosen* to have the respect of all the people, *chosen* as the highest judge over the entire nation. God has even spelled out the specifics you must do in order to protect your power and safeguard your strength. Soon, the awesome stories of your success spread like wildfire. Then, in walks Delilah!

You know you are not to reveal the secret of your strength, because God has said, "Don't tell." Yet you feel torn. You want to please God, but you also want to please Delilah, who has asked you to disclose the source of your strength. You try to resist, but the more you do, the more she cries and begs, prods, and pleads. Now you find yourself in *the Delilah Dilemma.* As you try to take care of her feelings, you cave in to her manipulation.

Finally, you confide that your strength is in your obedience to God in never, ever cutting your hair. Big mistake—a big mistake that leads to unimagined misery! Delilah tells the enemy Philistines, and they cut your hair and take you captive. However, your biggest mistake is not what you *said*, but what you *did—you let Delilah be your "god" instead of letting God be your God.* (See Judges 13–16.)

WHAT IS Dependency?

If Samson had not been so dependent on pleasing Delilah—if he had not been a "codependent people-pleaser"—he would not have lost his strength, his status, or his sight, nor would he have lost his spiritual insight. Ultimately, his *dependency* led to his *disobedience,* which in turn led to his *downfall.* In truth, *Samson's pride* caused his own downfall, for he prioritized the words of Delilah over the words of God.

> "Before his downfall
> a man's heart is proud,
> but humility comes before honor."
> (Proverbs 18:12)

▶ A **dependency** is a reliance on something or someone else for support or existence.

"I have to have this to live."

▶ A **dependency** can be either negative or positive, such as being dependent on cocaine versus being dependent on Christ.

"This is necessary for my life."

▶ A **dependency** can be an addiction to any object, behavior, or person that represents an underlying attempt to get emotional needs met.[1]

"I must do this to meet my needs to make me happy."

You Can Be Dependent on ...

OBJECTS

▶ A chemical addiction to drugs (alcohol, tobacco, cocaine)

▶ A sexual addiction to erotica items (pornography—magazines, videos—sex toys)

BEHAVIORS

▶ An addiction to behaviors that appear to be bad, those that are not widely socially acceptable and can be harmful (inappropriate sex, gambling, excessive spending, compulsive eating)

▶ An addiction to behaviors that appear to be good, those that are widely socially acceptable but may be equally harmful (perfectionism, workaholism, caregiving, even anorexia or bulimia)

PEOPLE

▶ A "love" addiction in which you feel that your identity is in another person. (A weak "love addict" is emotionally dependent on someone "strong.")

▶ A "savior" addiction in which you feel that your identity is in your ability to meet the needs of another person. (A strong "savior" needs to be needed by someone "weak.")

Because addictions provide a momentary "high," good feelings are associated with them. However, the book of Proverbs gives this poignant warning.

> "There is a way that seems right to a man, but in the end it leads to death." (Proverbs 14:12)

QUESTION: "What is wrong with people depending on people?"

ANSWER: We should have a healthy "interdependence" on others in the sense that we should value and enjoy each other, love and learn from each other, but we should not be totally dependent on each other. Essentially, this kind of relationship involves a healthy, mutual give-and-take, where neither person looks to the other to meet each and every need. However, many people have a *misplaced dependency* on others. These kinds of relationships are not healthy, for God intends for us to live in total dependence on Him.

Over and over, the Bible portrays how godly people learn to have a *strong dependence* on the Lord rather than a *weak dependence* on each other. The apostle Paul said we should …

"… not rely on ourselves but on God."
(2 Corinthians 1:9)

WHAT IS Codependency?[2]

Though the word *codependency* may be fairly new, the concept is age-old. We can certainly see how supposedly *strong Samson* violates his values by giving in to seemingly *dependent Delilah*. But this compromise of codependency was not his first. During the time of his seven-day wedding feast, Samson gave a riddle as a wager to the Philistines (the godless people of his new wife). His wife cried the entire time, *"You hate me! You don't really love me. You haven't told me the answer"* (Judges 14:16). On the final day of the feast, Samson was worn down and told his wife. Then, in turn, she told the Philistines.

As a result, violence and bloodshed ran rampant, only because *strong Samson* didn't act with the strength of his convictions. Instead, he became weak-willed, following the persistent pleading of his *weak wife*. Samson needed to …

> **"Be strong in the Lord**
> **and in his mighty power."**
> **(Ephesians 6:10)**

▶ Today, a *codependent* is anyone who is dependent on another person to the point of being controlled or manipulated by that person.

▶ The word *codependent* was first used in the 1970s to describe a family member living with an alcoholic. The prefix *co-* means "with" or "one associated with the action of another."

▶ *Codependency* became the word that describes the dysfunctional behavior of family members seeking to adapt to the destructive behavior of the alcoholic.

▶ *Codependency* is a relationship addiction. Just as the alcoholic is dependent on alcohol, the codependent is dependent on *being needed* by the alcoholic, or on being needed by someone who is dependent.

▶ The "enabler" is a *codependent* person who *enables* the alcoholic (or other dependent person) to continue with the addiction without drawing and maintaining boundaries. Codependency involves being too dependent on someone or something that cannot meet your needs.

Codependency can be compared to the sin of depending on false gods that are powerless to help or depending on a broken water well that won't hold water. It simply won't work!

"My people have committed two sins:
They have forsaken me,
the spring of living water,
and have dug their own cisterns,
broken cisterns that cannot hold water."
(Jeremiah 2:13)

QUESTION: "How can I know whether I'm an enabler?"

ANSWER: You are an *enabler* if you perpetuate another's destructive behavior by protecting that person from painful consequences that could actually serve as a motivation for change.

▶ The *enabling parent* allows the teenager's drug habit to continue with no repercussions, even to the detriment of other family members.

▶ The *enabling wife* calls her husband's boss to say that he has the flu when in fact he has a hangover.

Ask yourself, How many lies have I told to protect the reputation of the one with the destructive habit? The Bible has strong words to say about those who protect the guilty.

> "Whoever says to the guilty, 'You are innocent'—peoples will curse him and nations denounce him."
> (Proverbs 24:24)

WHAT ARE Common Codependent Relationships?

In a codependent relationship, one person is seen as *weak* and the other as *strong*. The weak one appears totally dependent on the strong one. But the one who appears strong is actually weak because of the excessive need to be needed by the weak one. In fact, the strong one needs for the weak one to stay weak, which in turn keeps the strong one feeling strong.

The ultimate solution—God's solution—for both of these *weak* persons is not to try to draw strength from each other, but rather to derive their strength from God. The Bible says ...

> "He gives strength to the weary and increases the power of the weak."
> (Isaiah 40:29)

Common Codependent Relationships

▶ A *wife* is excessively helpless around her *husband*, and the husband needs his wife to stay helpless.

▶ A *husband* is excessively needy in how he relates to his *wife,* and the wife needs him to stay needy.

▶ A *student* is excessively tied to a *teacher,* and the teacher needs the student to stay tied.

▶ A *child* is excessively pampered by the *parent*, and the parent needs the child to stay in need of pampering.

▶ A *parent* is excessively protected by the *child*, and the child needs the parent to stay in need of protection.

▶ An *employee* is excessively entangled with an *employer,* and the employer needs the employee to stay entangled.

▶ A *friend* is excessively fixated on another *friend,* and that person needs the friend to stay fixated.

▶ A *counselee* is excessively clinging to a *counselor,* and the counselor needs the counselee to continue clinging.

- ▶ A *disciple* is excessively dependent on a *discipler,* and the discipler needs the disciple to stay dependent.

- ▶ A *victim* is excessively vulnerable to a *victimizer,* and the victimizer needs the victim to stay vulnerable.

- ▶ A *layperson* is excessively leaning on a *spiritual leader,* and the leader needs the layperson to continue leaning.

When we have a *misplaced dependency,* we have a misplaced trust. We are excessively trusting in the relationship to provide more than God intended. The Psalms describe a misplaced trust:

> "Some trust in chariots
> and some in horses, but we trust
> in the name of the our God."
> (Psalm 20:7)

QUESTION: "When I was a struggling addict, my wife held our home together. Now that I have truly changed, why is she continually upset and threatening divorce?"

ANSWER: You changed the dynamic! After an alcoholic becomes healthy and whole, the *strong* codependent mate is no longer needed in the same way. The new dynamic changes the balance in the relationship. The strong one, who no longer feels needed in the same way, could choose to divorce and remarry another needy mate in order to feel needed again. Obviously, divorce is *not* the solution. For both of you to become emotionally balanced and spiritually healthy *is* the solution. Just as every alcoholic needs to overcome alcoholism, every codependent needs to overcome codependency. The Bible says ...

"Do not conform any longer
to the pattern of this world,
but be transformed by
the renewing of your mind.
Then you will be able to test and
approve what God's will is—his good,
pleasing and perfect will."
(Romans 12:2)

QUESTION: "In the parent-child relationship, what is the difference between *bonding* and *enmeshment*?"

ANSWER:

▶ *Healthy bonding* occurs when parents are connected with their children by being God's instruments to meet their basic physical, emotional, and spiritual needs. With *healthy bonding*, nurturing flows naturally from parent to child, leaving the child emotionally fulfilled and whole.

▶ *Unhealthy enmeshment* occurs when parents need an *excessive connection* with their children in order to get their own emotional needs met. With *enmeshment*, nurturing flows unnaturally from child to parent, leaving the child emotionally drained and empty.

> "Children should not
> have to save up for their parents,
> but parents for their children."
> (2 Corinthians 12:14)

▶ *God wants you to depend on Him*—to totally rely on Him, not on people or things or self-effort.

"My salvation and my honor depend on God; he is my mighty rock, my refuge." (Psalm 62:7)

▶ *God wants you to depend on Him*—to believe that He will meet all of your needs. You can safely reveal your hurts, your fears, and your needs to God. He will be your Need-Meeter.

"The LORD will guide you always; he will satisfy your needs in a sun-scorched land and will strengthen your frame. You will be like a well-watered garden, like a spring whose waters never fail." (Isaiah 58:11)

▶ *God wants you to depend on Him*—to trust in Him to take care of your loved ones.

"Trust in him at all times, O people; pour out your hearts to him, for God is our refuge." (Psalm 62:8)

▶ *God wants you to depend on Him*—to rely on Christ, whose life in you will enable you to overcome any destructive dependency.

"The one [Christ] who is in you is greater than the one [Satan] who is in the world." (1 John 4:4)

QUESTION: "What is the difference between a codependent marriage and a healthy marriage?"[3]

ANSWER:

▶ *An Unhealthy, Codependent Marriage*

- The *weak spouse* has a deep-seated need for security and continually looks to the *strong spouse* to meet all needs. This means that the *weak one* stays weak.

- The supposedly *strong spouse* has a deep-seated need for significance and tries to meet all the needs of the *weaker partner* in order to make that mate dependent on the relationship.

▶ *A Healthy, Interdependent Marriage*

- Each emphasizes the other's strengths and encourages the other partner to overcome personal weaknesses.

- Each encourages the other to be dependent on the Lord, while being responsive to the legitimate needs of the other.

"Each of you should look not only
to your own interests, but also to
the interests of others."
(Philippians 2:4)

CHARACTERISTICS OF CODEPENDENCY

Can children be *conditioned* to be codependent? Clearly, yes. In the Bible, Rebekah shows a blatant bias toward her second-born son, Jacob, because he stays close to hearth and home. Meanwhile, Isaac favors his firstborn son, Esau, because he has prowess in hunting.

Since no two children have identical skills, all children should be recognized for their differences and respected for their distinctiveness. Oh, but Rebekah does not love in this way! She becomes obsessed. Thus, the conniving begins. Rebekah wants Jacob to receive "the birthright of the firstborn" (which unquestionably belongs to Esau). She becomes determined to deceive her husband so that he will give it to Jacob. Because of the *enmeshed relationship* between Rebekah and Jacob, she finds it easy to persuade her son to defraud his father. She plots. She schemes. She secretly plans. Rebekah coaches Jacob to cover his hands with the skin of a young goat so that they will feel like the hands of his brother. She even dresses Jacob in Esau's clothes. Because of old age and weak eyes, father Isaac is fooled.

Although the scheme is a success, Jacob is found out and flees for his life. But alas, he does not escape his *passive dependency*. All too soon, he again becomes manipulated by others. His father-in-law and his own two wives are crafty and cunning. Meanwhile, he feels conned and controlled. Such is the misery in adulthood when one is enmeshed in childhood. (See Genesis chapters 27–30.)

WHO ARE Codependent People?

Codependent people may appear capable and self-sufficient, yet in reality they are insecure, self-doubting, and in need of approval. This need for approval results in an *excessive sense of responsibility* and a dependence on *people-pleasing performance*. However, the Bible says our primary focus should not be on pleasing people, but rather on pleasing God.[4]

"We instructed you how to live in order to please God, as in fact you are living. Now we ask you and urge you in the Lord Jesus to do this more and more."
(1 Thessalonians 4:1)

The Codependent Person Profile

Think about the person with whom you are closely involved and consider if any of these statements are reflections of you.

☐ I feel responsible for the feelings, needs, and actions of the other person.

☐ I try to fix the problems of this person, even to the detriment of my own well-being.

☐ I can discern the thoughts of this person but cannot identify my own.

☐ I know the feelings and needs of this person but do not know my own.

☐ I do things for others that they are capable of doing for themselves.

☐ I feel angry when my help is not wanted.

☐ I tend to be rigid and judgmental in the eyes of others.

☐ I judge myself more harshly than I judge others.

☐ I deny my own feelings and needs—so I've been told.

☐ I feel guilty when I stand up for myself.

☐ I feel good about giving but have difficulty receiving.

☐ I try to be perfect in order to avoid anger or criticism.

☐ I look for my worth in the approval of others.

☐ I find that I am attracted to needy people and that needy people are attracted to me.

WHAT IS a Codependent Relationship?

The classic codependent relationship is typically characterized by an emotionally *weak person* who feels the need to be connected to an emotionally *strong person*. The so-called strong one is actually weak because of the need to be needed. Both are insecure and become entangled in a web of emotional bondage. The two combine to produce a destructive cycle of manipulation and control, draining joy and happiness out of life. Because this destructive dynamic is often subconscious, both parties can feel innocent of any wrongdoing. Yet, God knows that their self-absorbed motives are consumed with trying to fill an empty emotional bucket that has no bottom.[5]

"All a man's ways seem innocent to him, but motives are weighed by the LORD."
(Proverbs 16:2)

- Both feel a loss of personal identity.
- Both violate their consciences.
- Both have difficulty establishing healthy, intimate relationships.
- Both struggle with low self-worth.
- Both control and manipulate.
- Both have difficulty setting boundaries.
- Both become jealous and possessive.
- Both fear abandonment.
- Both experience extreme ups and downs.
- Both are in denial.
- Both have a false sense of security.
- Both usually have one other addiction besides the relationship.
- Both feel trapped in the relationship.

QUESTION: "Is a friendship codependent when two friends depend on one another?"

ANSWER: No, if the friendship is interdependent (reciprocal with balanced sharing), then it is healthy. If the friendship is codependent (out of balance), then it is unhealthy.

"As iron sharpens iron, so one man sharpens another." (Proverbs 27:17)

▶ *An Unhealthy, Codependent Friendship*

- One friend is weak and troubled; the other friend is strong and competent. (There is an imbalance of power and of give-and-take.)

- One friend desires freedom to enjoy other significant relationships but is fearful of doing so. The other friend desires exclusivity and becomes easily jealous or threatened.

- Both may put the other friend in the place of Christ, and neither is bettered by the friendship.

▶ *A Healthy, Interdependent Friendship*

- Both come together as equals with a balance of power and of give-and-take.

- Both pursue and enjoy other significant relationships and avoid exclusivity.

- Both friends are better because of each other. Each strengthens the other spiritually.

Biblical Illustration: During a difficult time in David's life, his dearest friend, Jonathan, didn't try to draw David to himself. Instead, the Bible says, *"Jonathan ... helped him [David] find strength in God."* (1 Samuel 23:16)

QUESTION: "As an employee, how can I keep codependency out of my workplace?"

ANSWER: Don't be afraid to establish and maintain appropriate boundaries.

- Don't try to be your employer's "all-in-all"—the one who will always do everything.
- Don't be controlled by manipulation and fear.
- Don't let staying late be a detriment to your God-given, personal priorities. If the work load is too great to accomplish what you have been hired to do in the time allowed, you could express an accurate picture to your employer in this way: "Mr. (employer's name), thank you for the opportunity to work on this assignment. We seem to have run into a problem. You have employed me to be here 40 hours a week; however, there is at least 100 hours of work to be done. How do you want me to prioritize my tasks and utilize my 40 hours this week?"
- Don't be afraid to say *no* when it's appropriate to say *no*.

> "Let your 'Yes' be 'Yes,'
> and your 'No,' 'No.'"
> (Matthew 5:37)

QUESTION: "Should I date a woman who is secure, confident, and competent or someone who is insecure, from a difficult background, and really needs me?"

ANSWER: You can be a knight in shining armor and rescue a damsel in distress. But once you have rescued her and she goes on with her life, she will not value you as a person—only as a rescuer. You want to be wanted because you are loved, not because of emotional unhealthiness.

- Someone who is emotionally healthy can love you out of strength and will be able to accept you unconditionally and offer you security in a relationship.

- Someone who is emotionally needy is typically self-focused and limited in ability to be sensitive to the needs of others. Emotionally needy people are more often "takers" than "givers" in relationships and "use people up" emotionally.

Seek someone with emotional maturity and spiritual wisdom, someone who can help you to grow more and more in your relationship with the Lord.

"He who walks with the wise grows wise." (Proverbs 13:20)

Take the Codependency Checklist Test

Are you unsure about someone who is significant in your life? Is it possible that you are in a relationship that others would call "codependent"? If so, how would you know? Read through the Codependency Checklist and make a check mark (√) by what is applicable to you.

☐ Do you struggle with feeling loved; therefore, you look for ways to be needed?

☐ Do you want to throw all of your energy into helping someone else?

☐ Do you have difficulty saying "No" when you should say "Yes," and say "Yes" when you should say "No"?

☐ Do you feel compelled to take charge of another person's crisis?

☐ Do you feel drawn to others who seem to need to be rescued from their problems?

☐ Do you have difficulty setting and keeping boundaries?

☐ Do you find it difficult to identify and express your true feelings?

☐ Do you rely on the other person to make most of the decisions in your relationship?

☐ Do you feel lonely, sad, and empty when you are alone?

☐ Do you feel threatened when the other person spends time with someone else?

- ☐ Do you think the other person's opinion is more important than your opinion?
- ☐ Do you refrain from speaking in order to keep peace?
- ☐ Do you fear conflict because the other person could abandon you?
- ☐ Do you become defensive about your relationship with the other person?
- ☐ Do you feel "stuck" in the relationship with the other person?
- ☐ Do you feel that you have lost your personal identity in order to "fit into" the other person's world?
- ☐ Do you feel controlled and manipulated by the other person?
- ☐ Do you feel used and taken advantage of by the other person?
- ☐ Do you plan your life around the other person?
- ☐ Do you prioritize your relationship with the other person over your relationship with the Lord?

If you responded with a "yes" to four or more of these questions, you may be involved in a codependent relationship!

When we find ourselves in unhealthy patterns of relating, we need to change our focus, change our goals, and change what is hindering us from running the race God has planned for us. Our primary focus should be not on a person but on Jesus. (See Hebrews 12:1)

CAUSES OF CODEPENDENCY

What draws people into destructive, codependent relationships? The answer is most often found in their childhood pain—a past pain that impacts their adult choices. In reality, codependent people are grown-ups who have never grown up.

The Bible refers to immature grown-ups by using the analogy of infants feeding on milk instead of on solid food.

"Though by this time
you ought to be teachers,
you need someone to teach you
the elementary truths of God's word all
over again. You need milk,
not solid food!
Anyone who lives on milk,
being still an infant, is not acquainted
with the teaching about righteousness."
(Hebrews 5:12–13)

All children progress through five developmental stages on their way to maturity and adulthood. God designed the family to provide the necessary structure for the healthy completion of each of these stages. If as children we fail to progress successfully from one certain stage to another, our development will be stunted at that stage, and we will grow up to be emotionally immature adults. We will develop adult bodies, but—like children—we will be underdeveloped emotionally. As a result, we will be inclined to be drawn into codependent, needy relationships. Out of tender concern for the protection of children, Jesus gave this general, but strong, warning to adults:

"If anyone causes one of these little ones who believe in me to sin, it would be better for him to have a large millstone hung around his neck and to be drowned in the depths of the sea."
(Matthew 18:6)

Five Stages of Childhood Development

God bestows on parents the major responsibility of nurturing their children so that they will not be *love-starved*—an emotional state that sets them up to "look for love in all the wrong places."

1 The Helpless Stage

Babies need to bond with their parents because they are helpless and totally dependent for all of their basic needs (including the three inner needs for love, for significance, and for security).[7] If your parents did not meet your needs, you may have grown into a needy adult who feels "empty" inside—as if there is a hole in your heart.

2 The Pushing Away Stage

Toddlers need to begin to push away from their parents as a way of exploring their environment and setting boundaries. If your parents did not allow separation, you may have grown into an adult who manipulates others in order to gain some sense of control.

3 The Conflict Stage

Young children need to learn proper ways of resolving conflict as they begin to test their parents' rules. If you did not learn healthy conflict resolution skills, you may have grown into an adult who lacks problem-solving skills in your adult relationships.

4 The Independent Stage

Preadolescent children need to grow in independence, but they still need direction and support from their parents. If your parents stifled your assertiveness, you may have grown into a needy, unassertive adult who is dependent on others to validate you.

5 The Sharing Stage

Adolescents need to learn mutual give-and-take and even sacrificial sharing from their parents as they begin to pursue involvement within their own groups. If you did not see a healthy give-and-take between your parents or see ways of sacrificially helping others, you may have grown into a self-focused adult who forms unequal relationships in order to feel some sense of significance.

Children who grow up being emotionally needy and who are not allowed to learn the skills necessary for forming healthy, adult relationships never learn healthy independence. They have difficulty speaking the truth, asking for what they want, and setting boundaries. They become codependent adults who are *addicted to unhealthy relationships* because they never learned anything different. Ultimately, they are desperately trying to finish what they started in infancy—to grow up!

QUESTION: "As a parent, how can I keep my children from having an unhealthy dependence on me?"

ANSWER:

▶ Teach your children to pray about their decisions and to depend on God to guide them.

▶ Begin early to train your children to make their own decisions. For example, early on, allow them to choose between two or three options regarding the clothing they would like to wear.

▶ Praise your children for making good decisions—they will want to repeat actions that are praiseworthy.

- ▶ Allow your children to experience the repercussions of making bad decisions. Rather than finding a way to rescue them, maintain the boundary line—some of the most memorable lessons are learned the hard way.

- ▶ Teach your children the practical principles of decision making in regard to age-appropriate topics, such as boundaries, chores, friends, curfews, money, dating, and goals.

- ▶ Encourage your children to develop friendships with other children and to learn to give and take in relationships.

- ▶ Teach your children to take care of their possessions, to perform routine household chores, and to prepare meals.

- ▶ Show your children how to budget their money and how to establish spending priorities.

- ▶ Enroll your children in group activities or clubs that will expose them to new experiences, enhance their life skills, and develop their self-confidence.

- ▶ Identify your child's strengths and find avenues in which your child can succeed in developing those strengths.

"Train a child in the way he should go,
and when he is old
he will not turn from it."
(Proverbs 22:6)

God meant for us to grow. By God's design, you can change and grow in maturity. You can have mature relationships. By God's power, what has been ravaged can be restored. What has been ruined can be redeemed. Ask the Lord to transform your mind with His truth. Realize that the tree rooted in truth will bear much fruit.

"He is like a tree
planted by streams of water,
which yields its fruit in season
and whose leaf does not wither.
Whatever he does prospers."
(Psalm 1:3)

Have you wondered why some people go from one bad relationship to another? Your friend escapes one "controller" only to be attracted to another "controller." Why move from one negative relationship to another? Have you been caught in the cycle yourself? If so, you may have spoken these perplexing words of the apostle Paul.

> "What I do is not the good I want to do;
> no, the evil I do not want to do—
> this I keep on doing." (Romans 7:19)

What Childhood Setup Leads to Adult *Love Addiction*?

▶ As a child, I had a "love bucket" that was empty.

No one sets out to be emotionally addicted to another person, to constantly crave love from another person. These cravings were created in childhood because there was "no water in the well"—their "love buckets" were and still are empty. They are truly *love-starved*. When unloved children receive a rare moment of attention or affection from their unloving parents, the result is both exhilarating and confusing.

They feel confused as to why they can't be consistently loved, and they become fixated on how to get that feeling of love again. Rejected children live for any moment of acceptance. Any hint of love becomes an emotional high that temporarily relieves their pain. These children may become adult *love addicts* because they ...

- did not receive enough positive affirmation as children.
- grew up feeling unloved, insignificant, and insecure.
- experienced a traumatic separation or a lack of bonding.
- felt and continue to feel intense sadness and a profound loss at being abandoned.
- experienced repeated rejection from their parents.
- felt and continue to feel extreme fear, helplessness, and emptiness.

▶ As an adult, I find that my "love bucket" has holes in it.

Children with empty "love buckets" create a fantasy about some "savior" who will remove their fear and finally make them feel whole. But no matter how much love they receive, it's not enough because they themselves are not whole.

As adults, they are still emotionally needy "children" who …

- believe that being loved by someone—anyone—is the solution to their emptiness.

- enter relationships believing they cannot take care of themselves.

- assign too much value and power to the other person in a relationship.

- have tremendously unrealistic expectations of the other person.

- try to "stick like glue" to the other person in order to feel connected.

- live in fear that those who truly love them will ultimately leave them.

The plight of a *love addict* would seem without solution were it not for the Lord, who is the only true *Savior*, the One who loves them unconditionally and eternally. The Bible gives this assurance:

"I have loved you
with an everlasting love;
I have drawn you with loving-kindness."
(Jeremiah 31:3)

THE CYCLE OF THE *WEAK ONE*[8]
Scenario #1

A woman appears *weak* because as a child her emotional needs were never met. She fantasizes about her "knight in shining armor," who will one day sweep her away into romantic bliss. This *love addict* constantly yearns for someone to "complete" her as a person. She is drawn to "caregivers," yet at the same time, she is terrified at the thought of true intimacy.

THE CYCLE OF THE *STRONG ONE*[9]
Scenario #2

A man appears *strong* because as a child he was in an *enmeshed relationship* with his mother. He was his mother's "caregiver" and surrogate husband. (His father was emotionally or physically absent.) Now, as an adult, he is drawn to women who need to be "taken care of," but he is terrified at the thought of being smothered again.

Codependent relationships are formed by two people who are addicted to each other, but who are in denial about their addiction. Both the **weak** and **strong** persons can be either male or female. Both have *abandonment* issues and *enmeshment* issues. They generally flip-flop between being the *weak one* and the *strong one*—sometimes even within the same relationship. The intensity of their relationship and the intensity of their pain are immense as they swing from one extreme to the other—from suffocating one another to distancing from one another. They fail to focus on this simple, but wise, counsel:

"Avoid all extremes." (Ecclesiastes 7:18)

QUESTION: "Why do I keep getting into codependent relationships? I'm now wondering whether it is possible for me ever to break free and stay free?"

ANSWER: When two people are in a codependent relationship, each has a history of feeling both abandoned and controlled. First, recognize how afraid you are of being abandoned, and then realize how you resent being controlled. Your relationship is intense and unstable, full of conflict and chaos, with repeated cycles of "come close" and "go away." Oddly enough, you cannot live peaceably together or apart. You are caught in the destructive ups and downs of codependency and feel you cannot get off the unrelenting roller coaster. But this is not true. When you apply the biblical steps to freedom, it is possible to be set free, because …

"With God all things are possible."
(Matthew 19:26)

If you live your life with a *misplaced dependency* on others, you will miss the extraordinary relationship God planned for you to have with Him—you may even miss salvation and heaven.

When God created you, He planned for you to enter into a tender, trusting relationship with Him, for He is so trustworthy that you can totally depend on Him to meet all of your needs. He designed you to live in dependence on Him—not on anyone else—to complete you, to fulfill you.

How to Begin Depending on God Alone

If you have struggled with codependency, God has a solution for you—a solution that can be spelled out in four points.

#1 God's Purpose for You is *Salvation.*

What was God's motive in sending Christ to earth? To condemn you?

No, to express His love for you by saving you!

"God so loved the world that he gave his one and only Son, that whoever

believes in him shall not perish but have eternal life. For God did not send his Son into the world to condemn the world, but to save the world through him." (John 3:16–17)

What was Jesus' purpose in coming to earth? To make everything perfect and to remove all sin?

No, to forgive your sins, empower you to have victory over sin, and enable you to live a fulfilled life!

"I [Jesus] have come that they may have life, and have it to the full." (John 10:10)

#2 Your Problem is *Sin*.

What exactly is sin?

Sin is living independently of God's standard—knowing what is right, but choosing wrong.

"Anyone, then, who knows the good he ought to do and doesn't do it, sins." (James 4:17)

What is the major consequence of sin?

Spiritual death, spiritual separation from God.

"The wages of sin is death, but the gift of God is eternal life in Christ Jesus our Lord." (Romans 6:23)

#3 God's Provision for You is the *Savior.*

Can anything remove the penalty for sin?

Yes. Jesus died on the cross to personally pay the penalty for your sins.

"God demonstrates his own love for us in this: While we were still sinners, Christ died for us." (Romans 5:8)

What is the solution to being separated from God?

Belief in Jesus Christ as the only way to God the Father.

"Jesus answered, 'I am the way and the truth and the life. No one comes to the Father except through me.'" (John 14:6)

#4 Your Part is *Surrender.*

Place your faith in (rely on) Jesus Christ as your personal Lord and Savior and reject your "good works" as a means of gaining God's approval.

"It is by grace you have been saved, through faith—and this not from yourselves, it is the gift of God—not by works, so that no one can boast." (Ephesians 2:8–9)

Give Christ control of your life, entrusting yourself to Him.

"Jesus said to his disciples, 'If anyone would

come after me, he must deny himself and take up his cross and follow me. For whoever wants to save his life will lose it, but whoever loses his life for me will find it. What good will it be for a man if he gains the whole world, yet forfeits his soul?'" (Matthew 16:24–26)

The moment you choose to believe in Him—entrusting your life to Christ—He gives you His Spirit to live inside you. Then the Spirit of Christ gives you His power to live the life that God has planned for you. If you want to be fully forgiven by God and become the person He created you to be, you can tell Him in a simple, heartfelt prayer like this:

PRAYER OF SALVATION

"God, I want a real relationship with You. I admit that many times I've chosen to go my own way instead of Your way. Please forgive me for my sins. Jesus, thank You for dying on the cross to pay the penalty for my sins. Come into my life to be my Lord and my Savior. Help me to depend on You alone to meet my needs. Through Your power, make me the person You created me to be. In Your holy name I pray. Amen."

What Can You Expect Now?

If you sincerely prayed this prayer, look at what God's Word says that He will do for you!

"The LORD will guide you always;
he will satisfy your needs
in a sun-scorched land and will
strengthen your frame.
You will be like a well-watered garden,
like a spring whose waters never fail."
(Isaiah 58:11)

Everyone is created with three God-given inner needs—the needs for love, for significance, and for security. If we expect or demand that another person meet all of our needs or if we become dependent on another person to do so, we have a *misplaced dependency*. The Bible makes it plain that ...

"God will meet all your needs according to his glorious riches in Christ Jesus."
(Philippians 4:19)

▶ WRONG BELIEF FOR THE DEPENDENT:

"I need to be connected to a *stronger* person who will provide me with a sense of love and emotional security."

▶ RIGHT BELIEF FOR THE DEPENDENT:

"While God often expresses His love through others, He doesn't want me to live my life depending on another person. I need to live dependently on Jesus, who will meet my needs, give me healthy relationships, and make my life fruitful." Jesus said, *"I am the vine; you are the branches. If a man* remains in me and I in him, he will bear much fruit; apart from me you can do nothing." (John 15:5)

▶ WRONG BELIEF FOR THE CODEPENDENT:

"I am responsible for meeting all the needs of this person whom I love, and that gives me a real sense of significance."

▶ RIGHT BELIEF FOR THE CODEPENDENT:

"If I try to meet all the needs of any other person, I'm taking the role that God alone should have. My need for significance cannot be met by pleasing another person, but it is met by pleasing God and finding my significance in Him."

"We make it our goal to please him [God]." (2 Corinthians 5:9)

QUESTION: "As a counselor, how can I keep my clients from developing an unrealistic dependency on me?"

ANSWER:

▶ Don't have a session without first praying for God's wisdom. Then let your client know that you will be depending on the discernment God will give you.

▶ Don't allow yourself to be your client's "savior"—there is only one Savior, and you are not Him!

▶ Don't always be available—you have other responsibilities that will need to be given high priority levels.

▶ Don't pull your client to yourself, but rather present and model how to have an intimate relationship with the Lord.

▶ Don't rely on your own sufficiency based on your education or experiences. Instead, rely on the Lord's sufficiency and encourage your client to do the same.

> "Blessed is he whose help
> is the God of Jacob, whose hope
> is in the LORD his God."
> (Psalm 146:5)

STEPS TO SOLUTION

The primary problem with codependency can be called "idolatry"—giving a greater priority to anything or anyone other than God Himself. Our God is the One who created you and who has a wonderful plan for your life. He is the Lord who loves you and knows how to fulfill you. If you are in a codependent relationship:

▶ Your *excessive care* causes you to compromise your convictions.

▶ Your *excessive loyalty* leaves you without healthy boundaries.

▶ Your *excessive "love"* allows you to say *yes* when you should say *no.*

However, our Maker and Master has the right to have primary rule in our hearts and over our lives. Any other substitute is simply idolatry. The Bible says …

"Love the LORD your God
with all your heart and with all your soul
and with all your strength."
(Deuteronomy 6:5)

Notice two thoughts in this passage that seem to be in opposition to one another.

> "If someone is caught in a sin,
> you who are spiritual
> should restore him gently.
> But watch yourself,
> or you also may be tempted.
> Carry each other's burdens,
> and in this way you will fulfill
> the law of Christ.
> If anyone thinks he is something
> when he is nothing, he deceives himself.
> Each one should test his own actions.
> Then he can take pride in himself,
> without comparing himself
> to somebody else,
> for each one should carry his own load."
> (Galatians 6:1–5)

Does Scripture Contradict Itself?

Verse 2 says, *"Carry each other's burdens,"* and verse 5 says, *"Each one should carry his own load."*

Since these two clear-cut directives seem contradictory to each other, which one is true? When you carefully analyze what is being said, there is no contradiction.

▶ Verse 1—Gently encourage another person to change from negative behavior, but beware of your own temptation.

▶ Verse 2—The Greek word for "burden" is *baros*, which means "weight," implying a load or something that is pressing heavily.[10] When you help carry what is too heavy for someone else to bear alone, your caring response fulfills the law of Christ.

▶ Verse 5—The Greek word for "load" is *phortion*, which means "something carried."[11] Clearly, when you carry what others *should* carry, you are not wise. You are not called by God to relieve others of their rightful responsibilities.

CONCLUSION: Those who are codependent try to get their needs met by *carrying loads that others should be carrying*. To move out of a codependent relationship, both individuals need to quit trying to be the other person's "all-in-all" and instead *encourage each other to take responsibility for their own lives and to live dependently on the strength of God.*

KEY VERSE TO MEMORIZE

No other verse in the Bible is better at helping us set our priorities straight, put our relationships in the right order. We must put "first things first" or else we, in our relationships, will never have the fulfillment that God has planned for us.

"Am I now trying to win the approval of men, or of God? Or am I trying to please men? If I were still trying to please men, I would not be a servant of Christ."
(Galatians 1:10)

Codependency does not flow from an unchangeable personality flaw or some genetic fluke. A codependent relationship is rooted in immaturity, a fact that should give great hope to those caught in its addictive cycle. While change is never easy, growing up is always within the grasp of anyone who desires to move from immaturity to maturity.

Any of us can move from codependency to a healthy, mutual give-and-take in our relationships. The key to change is *motivation*. What kind of motivation? When your pain in the relationship is greater than your *fear of abandonment*, the motivation for change is powerful. Moving away from the pain of codependency then becomes a matter of choice and commitment. If you feel that the relationship you are in is more a curse than a blessing—when it brings more death to your soul than life—this is motivation for change.

"I have set before you life and death,
blessings and curses.
Now choose life, so that you ... may love
the Lord your God, listen to his voice,
and hold fast to him."
(Deuteronomy 30:19–20)

▶**Confront the Fact That You Are Codependent.**[12]

- *Admit the truth to yourself.* Before you can be free from the grasp of codependency, you must be honest with yourself about your emotional addiction to another person.

- *Admit the truth to someone else.* Identify the beliefs and behaviors that have perpetuated your emotional addiction and share them with an objective, trusted friend.

- *Admit the truth to God.* Realize that your emotional addiction is a serious sin in the eyes of God. Choose now to confess it to Him.

"Confess your sins to each other and pray for each other so that you may be healed. The prayer of a righteous man is powerful and effective." (James 5:16)

▶**Confront the Consequences of Your Codependency.**

- *Accept responsibility* for how your past experiences and reactions have hurt your adult relationships (such as your becoming manipulative, controlling, possessive, or angry).

- *Accept responsibility* for the pain you have caused yourself because of your codependency (such as your becoming jealous, envious, selfish, or obsessive).

- *Accept responsibility* for the ways in which your codependency has weakened your relationship with God (such as a loss of quantity time, quality time, and intimacy with the Lord).

"He who conceals his sins does not prosper, but whoever confesses and renounces them finds mercy." (Proverbs 28:13)

▶ **Confront Your Painful Emotions.**

- *Understand* that you will have pain no matter what you choose. If you leave the codependent relationship, you will hurt, but if you stay, you will hurt. However, the only hope for future healing is leaving the codependent lifestyle.

- *Understand* that when the intensity of the relationship diminishes you will experience emotional "withdrawal" from the exhilarating highs.

- *Understand* that you will need the support of others to get you through the initial pain of withdrawal and to help you avoid anesthetizing your pain with a "secondary addiction."

"Perfume and incense bring joy to the heart, and the pleasantness of one's friend springs from his earnest counsel." (Proverbs 27:9)

▶ Confront Your "Secondary Addictions."[13]

- *Recognize* that, in an effort to numb the emotional pain of the relationship, codependency often leads to other addictions, such as a chemical dependency, sexual addiction, compulsive eating, or excessive spending.

- *Recognize* your "secondary addictions"; then seek counseling and spiritual support to overcome them.

- *Recognize* that recovery from a "secondary addiction" is dependent on recovery from your primary addiction.

"The heart of the discerning acquires knowledge; the ears of the wise seek it out." (Proverbs 18:15)

▶ Confront Your Current Codependent Relationship.[14]

- *Acknowledge* your codependent role in the relationship and cease relating through codependent patterns.

- *Acknowledge* your destructive behaviors. (Write them down.) Then replace them with constructive behaviors. (Write them down.)

- *Acknowledge* the natural pain of emotional withdrawal (common to the healing of addictions) and focus on God's supernatural purpose (conforming you to the character of Christ).

"Those God foreknew he also predestined to be conformed to the likeness of his Son." (Romans 8:29)

▶ **Confront Your Codependent Focus.**

- *Stop focusing* on what the other person is doing and start focusing on what you need to do in order to become emotionally healthy.

- *Stop focusing* on the other person's problems and start focusing on solving your own problems (those resulting from your neglect of people and projects in your life).

- *Stop focusing* on trying to change the other person and start focusing on changing yourself.

"The wisdom of the prudent is to give thought to their ways, but the folly of fools is deception." (Proverbs 14:8)

▶ Confront Your Codependent Conflicts.[15]

- *Do not* allow yourself to become trapped in heated arguments or to become emotionally hooked by the bad behavior of the other person. Instead, say to yourself several times, *I will not argue*—and then disengage from the conflict. Decide ahead of time that, when agitation begins, you will distance yourself.

- *Do not* defend yourself when you are unjustly blamed. Instead, say only once, "I'm sorry you feel that way. That doesn't reflect my heart."

- *Do not* be afraid to leave if the conflict continues. State, "I will be gone for a while." Then calmly walk away.

"Don't have anything to do with foolish and stupid arguments, because you know they produce quarrels." (2 Timothy 2:23)

▶ Confront Your Codependent Responses.[16]

- *Remind yourself* that "problem people" have the right to choose wrong. Don't react to their problem behavior—they are *independent* of you.

- *Remind yourself* not to return insult for insult—refuse to raise your voice.

- *Remind yourself* that your Christlike role is to respond with respect—even when others are disrespectful.

"Do not repay evil with evil or insult with insult, but with blessing, because to this you were called so that you may inherit a blessing. ... But do this with gentleness and respect, keeping a clear conscience, so that those who speak maliciously against your good behavior in Christ may be ashamed of their slander." (1 Peter 3:9, 15–16)

▶ **Confront What You Need to Leave in Order to Receive.**

- *Leave* your childhood and your dependent thinking. (*I can't live without you.*) Then enter into healthy adulthood. (*I want you in my life, but if something were to happen, I could still live without you.*) That is reality.

- *Leave* your immature need to be dependent on someone else and embrace your mature need to be dependent on the Lord, who will make you whole within yourself.

- *Leave* your fantasy relationships (thinking, *You are my "all-in-all"*) and instead nurture several balanced relationships of healthy give-and-take.

"Wounds from a friend can be trusted, but an enemy multiplies kisses." (Proverbs 27:6)

▶**Confront Your Need to Build Mature Non-Codependent Relationships.**

- *Establish* several interdependent relationships—not just one *exclusive* relationship. You need mature relationships in which your codependency issues can be resolved and your needs can be met in healthy ways.

- *Establish* emotionally balanced relationships without being *needy* of the extreme highs and lows of codependent relationships.

- *Establish* personal boundaries in all of your relationships, saying *no* when you need to say *no* and holding to your *no*.

"Let us ... go on to maturity." (Hebrews 6:1)

One effective way to confront codependent love relationships is by using the "written word." Spelling out your thoughts, feelings, and actions will actually distance them from you so that you can look at them. Putting your relationships on paper helps paint a more complete picture, which in turn enables you to gain insights and devise a recovery plan. Putting your life on paper is not easy, but until you are ready to take a close look at your *love addiction*, you cannot expect to change it.

Write down the history of your codependent love relationships. First ask the Spirit of God to bring to mind what you need to know and then to teach you what you need to do. He will give you both understanding and wisdom to know how to free yourself of the fettered addictions and how to live in His glorious freedom.[17]

> "He who gets wisdom
> loves his own soul;
> he who cherishes understanding
> prospers." (Proverbs 19:8)

Make a list of every person with whom you have had a codependent relationship. Think through your family and friends. Put each name at the top of a separate page and then answer the following questions for each relationship:

1. *Write out ...*

- How did you meet and how were you attracted to this person?
- How did you pursue and draw this person to you?
- How did you feel and what did you fantasize about this person?

Conclude by answering ...

- How do you think God felt about your choices?
- Realize that the Lord is ready to meet your deepest emotional needs. Yet, when we live with misplaced priorities, the Bible says we commit spiritual adultery.

"I have been grieved by their adulterous hearts, which have turned away from me, and by their eyes, which have lusted after their idols. They will loathe themselves for the evil they have done and for all their detestable practices." (Ezekiel 6:9)

2. *Write out ...*

- How did the relationship progress through various stages (Fascination, Fantasy, Fog, Fear, Forsaking, Fixation, Frenzy)?

- How did you feel in each stage?

- How did you act during each stage?

Conclude by answering ...

- How did you fail to involve God in your life during each stage?

- Realize how ready the Lord has been to intervene.

"When I came, why was there no one? When I called, why was there no one to answer? Was my arm too short to ransom you? Do I lack the strength to rescue you? By a mere rebuke I dry up the sea, I turn rivers into a desert; their fish rot for lack of water and die of thirst. I clothe the sky with darkness and make sackcloth its covering." (Isaiah 50:2–3)

3. *Write out ...*

- How did you become preoccupied with the relationship?

- How did you start neglecting yourself and start focusing on taking care of the other person?

- How did you come to expect that person to meet all of your needs?

Conclude by answering ...

- How did you start neglecting God and when did you stop relying on Him?

- Realize how ready the Lord has been to make you fruitful.

"I had planted you like a choice vine of sound and reliable stock. How then did you turn against me into a corrupt, wild vine?" (Jeremiah 2:21)

4. *Write out ...*

- How has this relationship replicated your painful childhood experiences?

- How were you mistreated in the relationship and how did you react?

- How does the relationship impact you today?

Conclude by answering ...

- How is God replacing (or wanting to replace) your self-destructive, love-addicted patterns with constructive, healthy, holy patterns?

- Realize how ready the Lord is to "re-parent" you in order to meet your deepest needs and heal your deepest hurts.

"Though my father and mother forsake me, the LORD will receive me." (Psalm 27:10)

5. *Write out ...*

- How have you experienced fear, envy, jealousy, abandonment, and anger in the relationship?

- How did you assign a higher priority to this person than to everything else?

- How have you made the person the focus of your thought life?

Conclude by answering ...

- How can you appropriate "the mind of Christ" in order to overcome destructive feelings and to live out of your resources in Christ?

- Realize how ready the Lord has been to give you His thinking.

"We have the mind of Christ."
(1 Corinthians 2:16)

6. *Write out ...*

- How do you feel about the person and the relationship now?

- How has your perspective changed?

- How did things, people, and circumstances become factors in changing your perspective?

Conclude by answering ...

- How do you think God has been involved in changing your perspective?
- Realize how ready the Lord is to complete His perfect plan for your life.

"Being confident of this, that he who began a good work in you will carry it on to completion until the day of Christ Jesus." (Philippians 1:6)

We all love to see pictures of babies and then to see their stairstep growth into young adulthood. Built within little, immature children is the ability to grow to maturity. Why should it be any less for immature adults? They too can move from their immaturity and develop mature relationships.

Once we understand the goal of each developmental stage for reestablishing healthy relationships, we can set out to accomplish those goals—without the aid of earthly parents. Many have done this by "taking the hand" of the heavenly Father and allowing Him to "re-parent" them. You too can do this by having a plan and then working your plan with the caring support of others. It is an enormously important journey with enormously gratifying rewards. This is the journey God intended for you to take from the beginning.

"Do not fear, for I am with you;
do not be dismayed, for I am your God. I
will strengthen you and help you;
I will uphold you with my righteous
right hand." (Isaiah 41:10)

▶ Make it your goal to develop an intimate relationship with God and to form interdependent relationships with significant people in your life.

- Commit to becoming actively involved in a group Bible study and in group prayer.

- Commit to reading God's Word on a daily basis and memorizing Scripture.

- Commit to finding an accountability group and a Christian "relationship mentor" who will be available to you, spend time with you on a regular basis, be honest with you, and coach you in your relationships.

"Let us not give up meeting together … but let us encourage one another." (Hebrews 10:25)

▶ Make a plan to move toward maturity in your relationships.

- Ask God to help you discern where you are stuck in the relationship developmental stages.

- Ask your mentor or another wise person to help you identify your relationship needs (for example, sharing, problem-solving, listening, negotiating).

- Ask your accountability group to hold you accountable to establish appropriate goals in order to meet each of your relationship needs.

"Perseverance must finish its work so that you may be mature and complete, not lacking anything." (James 1:4)

▶ Make your relationship with your parents complete.

- Choose to resolve any unhealthy patterns with your parents. Break any unhealthy bond and, if possible, establish mature, adult bonds with each parent.

- Choose to not be *emotionally enmeshed*, needy, or controlled by your parents. If necessary, separate yourself emotionally until you can respond in a healthy way with "no strings attached."

- Choose to identify and process your "family of origin" problems, forgive your offenders, and grieve your losses. Say, "That was then; this is now."

"Do not take revenge, my friends, but leave room for God's wrath, for it is written: 'It is mine to avenge; I will repay,' says the Lord." (Romans 12:19)

▶ Make a vow to be a person of integrity in thought, word, and deed.

- Learn to free yourself of any family secrets—refuse to carry them any longer.

- Learn to listen, to say *no*, to set boundaries, to give and receive, and to ask for what you need from people. Then practice, practice, practice these new, healthy patterns.

- Learn to feel your feelings, to express hurt, and to withdraw and think about what you need to do or say. Write out your action plan; rehearse it; then do it.

"Prepare your minds for action; be self-controlled; set your hope fully on the grace to be given you when Jesus Christ is revealed. As obedient children, do not conform to the evil desires you had when you lived in ignorance. But just as he who called you is holy, so be holy in all you do." (1 Peter 1:13–15)

▶ Make a new job description.

- My job is to discern the character of a person and to respond accordingly with maturity.

- My job is to be a safe person for my friends and family and to be present and attentive in my relationships.

- My job is to take care of myself and to be responsible for myself without hurting, punishing, attacking, getting even, or lying to myself or to others.

"I will maintain my righteousness and never let go of it; my conscience will not reproach me as long as I live." (Job 27:6)

▶ Make a new commitment to yourself.

- I will let go of the "old," self-centered me because I am growing into a "new," Christ-centered me.

- I will exchange the lies I've believed about myself for God's truth about me according to His Word.

- I will no longer betray myself by making immature choices, and I will redeem my past, bad choices by making good, mature choices.

"If anyone is in Christ, he is a new creation; the old has gone, the new has come!" (2 Corinthians 5:17)

▶ Make maturity, not emotional relationships, your highest goal.

- Focus on forming friendships in which you are free to learn, grow, and mature, not emotional attachments that lead to roller-coaster relationships.

- Focus on any potential relationships that might trigger your codependent tendencies and guard your heart from the emotional highs and lows.

- Focus on building relationships with trustworthy, mature Christians whose goal is Christlikeness.

- During a severe time of trial, David's dear friend, Jonathan *"helped him find strength in God."* (1 Samuel 23:16)

When you are behaving in a codependent way, you are trying to get your needs met through a drive to "do it all" or to be another person's "all-in-all." However, you can "travel the road to recovery" by *releasing* your desire to control or to change the person you love.

RELEASE

RECOGNIZE that you are overly dependent on a person and instead place your dependency on God.

Admit that your codependency is a sin.

- Pray that God will give you the desire to put Him first and to please Him in all your relationships.

- Determine to look to the Lord to meet your needs for love, for significance, and for security.

- Realize that God did not create you to meet all the needs of another person.

"Love the LORD your God with all your heart and with all your soul and with all your strength." (Deuteronomy 6:5)

EXAMINE your patterns of codependent thinking.

Don't believe that pleasing people is always Christlike.

- Don't think that you should always assume the role of peacemaker.
- Don't fear losing the love of others when you allow them to suffer the consequences of their negative actions.
- Don't say *yes* when you really believe you should say *no*.

"Surely you desire truth in the inner parts; you teach me wisdom in the inmost place." (Psalm 51:6)

LET GO of your "super responsible" mentality.

Confess that you are trying to be like God in the life of another person.

- Trust God to be actively working in the life of your loved one.
- Realize that you cannot *make* another person be dependable or responsible.
- Rest in God's sovereign control over all people, events, and circumstances.

"What you are doing is not good. You and these people who come to you will only wear yourselves out. The work is too heavy for you; you cannot handle it alone." (Exodus 18:17–18)

EXTEND forgiveness to those who have caused you pain.

Reflect on any type of abuse you have experienced in the past—verbal, emotional, physical, or sexual.

- What has been unjust and painful in your life?
- Whom do you need to forgive?
- Would you be willing to release this person and your pain to God?
- Choose to forgive again whenever your angry feelings resurface.

"Bear with each other and forgive whatever grievances you may have against one another. Forgive as the Lord forgave you." (Colossians 3:13)

Appropriate your identity in Christ.

Learn to live out of your resources in Christ Jesus.

- Know the truth: "I can be emotionally set free because Christ lives in me."

  *"If the Son **sets you free**, you will be free indeed."* (John 8:36)

- Believe the truth: "I can change my dependency on people through the power of Christ in me."

  *"I can do everything **through him** who gives me strength."* (Philippians 4:13)

- Appropriate the truth: "I will nurture only healthy, godly relationships because I have been given Christ's divine nature."

  *"His divine power has given us everything we need for life and godliness through our knowledge of him who called us by his own glory and goodness. Through these he has given us his very great and precious promises, so that through them you may participate in the **divine nature** and escape the corruption in the world caused by evil desires."* (2 Peter 1:3–4)

Set healthy boundaries.

Communicate the necessity for change.

"I realize that I have not been responding to you in a healthy way. I have been far too dependent on you to meet my needs. And I have sought to meet all of your needs. I am committed to having healthy relationships and to putting God first in my life. I know that I have had negative responses to you, and I intend to begin having positive responses by making decisions based on what is right in the eyes of God."

- Establish what you need to ask forgiveness for.

   "I realize I was wrong for _____ (not speaking up when I should have, not being the person I should have been in this relationship, etc.). Will you forgive me?"

- Establish what your limits of responsibility will be.

   "I feel responsible for _____. But I am not responsible for _____ (making you happy, making you feel significant, etc.). I want you to be happy, but I don't have the power to make you happy."

- Establish your limits of involvement.

"I want to do _____ with/for you, but I don't feel led by God to do _____."

"The prudent see danger and take refuge, but the simple keep going and suffer for it."
(Proverbs 27:12)

EXCHANGE your emotional focus for spiritual focus.

Make God and your spiritual growth your first priority.

- Attend an in-depth Bible study in order to learn the heart of God and to grow spiritually with the people of God.

- Memorize sections of Scripture in order to put God's Word in your heart and to learn the ways of God.

- Redirect your thoughts to the Lord and take "prayer walks" (talking out loud to the Lord as you walk regularly in your neighborhood or on a trail).

"Direct me in the path of your commands, for there I find delight. Turn my heart toward your statutes and not toward selfish gain. Turn my eyes away from worthless things; preserve my life according to your word."
(Psalm 119:35–37)

The cure for codependency is rooted in developing an ever-deepening relationship with the Lord. Your increased intimacy with Him will naturally conform you to His character. When you let the Lord live inside you, *you can live in His power.* This means that because Christ was not codependent, *you have His power to overcome codependency.*

"In this world you will have trouble. But take heart! I have overcome the world." (John 16:33)

PRAYER OF FORGIVENESS

*"God, You know the pain
I experienced in my past.
I don't want to keep carrying all this
pain for the rest of my life. I release* (list hurts) *into Your hands, and I ask You
to heal my emotional pain.
Lord, You know what* (name of person) *has done to hurt me. As an act of my
will, I choose to forgive* (name). *I take* (name) *off my emotional hook and put* (name) *onto Your emotional hook.
Thank You, Lord Jesus, for setting
me FREE. In Your holy name I pray.
Amen."*

CODEPENDENCY PRAYER

*"Lord Jesus, I renounce as a lie
the thought that I could ever be
truly abandoned or alone.*

*Thank You that You will
never abandon me
or leave me without support.*

*Thank You that no matter what I do
or what my circumstances,
no matter who is in my life
or not in my life,
You will be with me and
provide for my needs.*

*Thank You that Your plans for me
are for my good and that
You will carry them out.*

*Thank You that You are not
dependent on anything or anyone
other than Yourself to bring about
Your good intentions toward me.*

*I trust in You and You alone to
give me meaning and purpose and
fulfillment in life.*

*In Your holy name I pray,
Amen."*

Help for an Unhealthy Relationship

Releasing You

Releasing is not to stop loving you,
  but is to love enough to stop leaning on
  you.

Releasing is not to stop caring for you,
  but is to care enough to stop controlling
  you.

Releasing is not to turn away from you,
  but is to turn to Christ, trusting His control
  over you.

Releasing is not to harm you,
  but is to realize "my help" has been
  harmful.

Releasing is not to hurt you,
  but is to be willing to be hurt for healing.

Releasing is not to judge you,
  but is to let the divine Judge judge me.

Releasing is not to restrict you,
  but is to restrict my demands of you.

Releasing is not to refuse you,
  but is to refuse to keep reality from you.

Releasing is not to cut myself off from you,
  but is to prune the unfruitful away from you.

Releasing is not to prove my power over you,
  but is to admit I am powerless to change
  you.

Releasing is not to stop believing in you,
  but is to believe the Lord alone will build
  character in you.

Releasing you is not to condemn the past,
  but is to cherish the present and commit our
  future to God.

—June Hunt

My Commitment because of Christ in Me

Because Jesus lives in me
  … I will conquer codependency.

Because Christ was not a "people-pleaser"
  … I will not be a "people-pleaser."

Because Christ refused to compromise
  … I will not yield to compromise.

Because Christ kept healthy boundaries
  … I will keep healthy boundaries.

Because Christ stood up to pressure
  … I will not cave in to pressure.

Because Jesus lives in me
  … I will conquer codependency!

—June Hunt

"I have been crucified with Christ
and I no longer live, but *Christ lives in
me*. The life I live in the body, I live by
faith in the Son of God, who loved me
and gave himself for me."
(Galatians 2:20)

SCRIPTURES TO MEMORIZE

What does the Lord say about making people like **gods**, putting them before my relationship with Him?

*"You shall have no other **gods** before me."* (Exodus 20:3)

Can the **Son of God set you free** from a codependent relationship?

*"If the **Son sets you free**, you will be free indeed."* (John 8:36)

Doesn't God want me to **trust in** and **depend** on the **strength** of significant people?

*"This is what the LORD says: 'Cursed is the one who **trusts in** man, who **depends** on flesh for his **strength** and whose heart turns away from the LORD.'"* (Jeremiah 17:5)

How do I forgive **whatever grievances** I have toward someone who drains me emotionally?

*"Bear with each other and forgive **whatever grievances** you may have against one another. Forgive as the Lord forgave you."* (Colossians 3:13)

Am I to put my **trust in the Lord** or put my **confidence** in people?

*"Blessed is the man who **trusts in the Lord**, whose **confidence** is in him."* (Jeremiah 17:7)

Don't I need someone to **depend on** to be my **rock** of strength, **my refuge**?

*"My salvation and my honor **depend on** God; he is **my** mighty **rock**, **my refuge**."* (Psalm 62:7)

When someone pretends to need help, should I insist that he **carry his own load**?

*"Each one should test his own actions. Then he can take pride in himself, without comparing himself to somebody else, for each one should **carry his own load**."* (Galatians 6:4–5)

Is there something wrong with seeking to **please men** in order to **win their approval**?

*"Am I now trying to **win the approval** of men, or of God? Or am I trying to **please men**? If I were still trying to please men, I would not be a servant of Christ."* (Galatians 1:10)

Can God **give me strength** to break away from a codependent relationship?

*"I can do everything through him who **gives me strength**."* (Philippians 4:13)

Why should I **cast** my **anxiety on the Lord** when I'm trying to become more independent?

*"**Cast** all your **anxiety on him** because he cares for you."* (1 Peter 5:7)

NOTES

1. Robert Hemfelt, Frank Minirth, and Paul Meier, *Love Is a Choice* (Nashville: Thomas Nelson, 1989), 11–12.

2. Melody Beattie, *Codependent No More: How to Stop Controlling Others and Start Caring for Yourself* (New York: Harper, 1987), 29–30; Jan Silvious, *Please Don't Say You Need Me: Biblical Answers for Codependency* (Grand Rapids: Pyranee, 1989), 9–10.

3. Silvious, *Please Don't Say You Need Me*, 45–119.

4. Beattie, *Codependent No More*, 35–47.

5. Hemfelt, Minirth, and Meier, *Love Is a Choice*, 20–28.

6. John Bradshaw, *How Childhood Development Stages Effect* [sic] *Adult Relationships*, VHS, Part 1 and 2, Linkletter Films (Nimco, 2000), distributed as *The Sources of Love*, vol. 1 and *The Work of Love*, vol. 2.

7. Lawrence J. Crabb, Jr., *Understanding People: Deep Longings for Relationship*, Ministry Resources Library (Grand Rapids: Zondervan, 1987), 15–16; Robert S. McGee, *The Search for Significance*, 2nd ed. (Houston, TX: Rapha, 1990), 27–30.

8. Pia Mellody, Andrea Wells Miller, and J. Keith Miller, *Facing Love Addiction: Giving Yourself the Power to Change the Way You Love* (New York: Harper San Francisco, 1992), 20–48.

9. Mellody, Miller, and Miller, *Facing Love Addiction*, 20–48.

10. W. E. Vine, Merrill F. Unger, and William White, Jr., *Vine's Expository Dictionary of Biblical Words* (Nashville: Thomas Nelson, 1985), s.v., "Burden, Burdened, Burdensome."

11. Vine, Unger, and White, *Vine's Expository Dictionary of Biblical*, s.v., "Burden, Burdened, Burdensome."

12. Hemfelt, Minirth, and Meier, *Love is a Choice*, 180–184.

13. Mellody, Miller, and Miller, *Facing Love Addiction*, 78–79.

14. Mellody, Miller, and Miller, *Facing Love Addiction*, 196–198.

15. Mellody, Miller, and Miller, *Facing Love Addiction*, 90–92.

16. Mellody, Miller, and Miller, *Facing Love Addiction*, 90–92.

17. Mellody, Miller, and Miller, *Facing Love Addiction*, 94–100; Valerie J. McIntyre, *Sheep in Wolves' Clothing*, 2nd ed. (Grand Rapids: Baker, 1996), 137–144; Hemfelt, Minirth, and Meier, *Love is a Choice*, 187–191; Rich Buhler, *Pain and Pretending*, rev. and exp. ed. (Nashville: Thomas Nelson, 1991), 160–164.

SELECTED BIBLIOGRAPHY

Arterburn, Stephen. *Addicted to "Love": Understanding Dependencies of the Heart: Romance, Relationships, and Sex*. 2nd ed. Ann Arbor, MI: Vine, 1996.

Arterburn, Stephen, and Tim Timmons. *Hooked on Life: How to Totally Recover from Addictions & Codependency*. Nashville: Oliver Nelson, 1985.

Beattie, Melody. *Beyond Codependency: and Getting Better All the Time*. Grand Rapids: Harper/Hazelden, 1989.

Beattie, Melody. *Codependent No More: How to Stop Controlling Others and Start Caring for Yourself*. New York: Harper/Hazelden, 1987.

Berry, Carmen Renee, and Mark Lloyd Taylor. *Loving Yourself as Your Neighbor: A Recovery Guide for Christians Escaping Burnout and Codependency*. Grand Rapids: Harper & Row, 1990.

Bobgan, Martin, and Deidre Bobgan. *12 Steps to Destruction: Codependency/Recovery Heresies*. Santa Barbara, CA: EastGate, 1991.

Bradshaw, John. *How Childhood Development Stages Effect Adult Relationships*. VHS. Linkletter Films. Distributed as *The Sources of Love*, vol. 1 and *The Work of Love*, vol. 2. Nimco, 2000.

Buhler, Rich. *Love: No Strings Attached*. Nashville: Thomas Nelson, 1987.

Buhler, Rich. *Pain and Pretending.* Rev and expanded ed. Nashville: Thomas Nelson, 1991.

Cloud, Henry, and John Townsend. *The Mom Factor Workbook: Dealing with the Mother You Had, Didn't Have, or Still Contend With.* Grand Rapids: Zondervan, 1997.

Crabb, Lawrence J., Jr. *Understanding People: Deep Longings for Relationship.* Ministry Resources Library. Grand Rapids: Zondervan, 1987.

Groom, Nancy. *From Bondage to Bonding: Escaping Codependency Embracing Biblical Love.* Colorado Springs, CO: NavPress, 1991.

Ells, Alfred. *One-Way Relationships.* Nashville: Thomas Nelson, 1990.

Hammond, Frank D. *Soul Ties.* Rev. ed. Plainview, TX: Children's Bread Ministry, 1995.

Hemfelt, Robert, Frank Minirth, and Paul Meier. *Love Is A Choice.* Nashville: Thomas Nelson, 1989.

Hunt, June. *Healing the Hurting Heart: Answers to Real Letters from Real People.* Dallas: Hope For The Heart, 1995.

Hunt, June. *Seeing Yourself Through God's Eyes.* Dallas: Hope For The Heart, 1989.

McGee, Robert S. *The Search for Significance.* 2nd ed. Houston, TX: Rapha, 1990.

McIntyre, Valerie J. *Sheep in Wolves' Clothing: How Unseen Need Destroys Friendship and Community and What to Do about It.* 2nd ed. Grand Rapids: Baker, 1996.

Mellody, Pia. *Facing Codependence: What It Is, Where It Comes from, How It Sabotages Our Lives.* San Francisco, CA: Perennial, 1989.

Mellody, Pia, Andrea Wells Miller, and J. Keith Miller. *Facing Love Addiction: Giving Yourself the Power to Change the Way You Love: The Love Connection to Codependence.* New York: Harper San Francisco, 1992.

Playfair, William L., and George Bryson. *The Useful Lie.* Wheaton, IL: Crossway, 1991.

Rinck, Margaret J. *Can Christians Love Too Much?: Breaking the Cycle of Codependency.* Grand Rapids: Pyranee, 1989.

Silvious, Jan. *Please Don't Say You Need Me: Biblical Answers for Codependency.* Grand Rapids: Pyranee, 1989.

Silvious, Jan, and Carolyn Capp. *Please Remind Me How Far I've Come: Reflections for Codependents.* Grand Rapids: Daybreak, 1990.

Stiles, Steven E. *Recovery for Codependency.* Spiritual Discovery Series. Springfield, MO: Radiant Life, 1997.

Viorst, Judith. *Necessary Losses: The Loves, Illusions, Dependencies, and Impossible Expectations that All of Us Have to Give Up in Order to Grow.* New York: Fireside, 1986.

Whiteman, Tom, and Randy Petersen. *Victim of Love?: How You Can Break the Cycles of Bad Relationships.* Colorado Springs, CO: Piñon, 1998.

June Hunt's HOPE FOR THE HEART booklets are biblically-based, and full of practical advice that is relevant, spiritually-fulfilling and wholesome. Each topic presents scriptural truths and examples of real-life situations to help readers relate and integrate June's counseling guidance into their own lives. Practical for individuals from all walks of life, this new booklet series invites readers into invaluable restoration, emotional health, and spiritual freedom.

HOPE FOR THE HEART TITLES

www.aspirepress.com

Display available for churches and ministries.

www.aspirepress.com